GOBLETS 1

S. T. Millard

Photographs by C. J. Boeger, Topeka, Kansas

Wallace-Homestead Book Company
Box BI
Des Moines, Iowa 50304

PRINTED IN U. S. A.

GOBLETS

A book intended primarily to bring
before the collector and dealer an ac-
curate knowledge of the major por-
tions of goblets existing and to estab-
lish a terminology for them that will
be at once effective and uniform.

By

S. T. MILLARD, M.D.

SECOND EDITION

*Written
in 1938*

FOREWORD

GOBLETS I and GOBLETS II by the Late Dr. S. T. Millard were originally published in 1938 and 1940 respectively. For many years these books have been out of print and obtainable only in the rare book market at premium prices. Pattern glass collectors have always considered the "Millard" books to be invaluable for history and rare pattern identification. Now, thanks to the offset method of printing, WALLACE-HOMESTEAD has again made these books available to the general public, along with Dr. Millard's definitive study of milk glass, OPAQUE GLASS.

The reader should keep in mind that printing methods at the time of original publication were not what they are today. Some of the illustrations are not of the clarity they would be if taken and printed with modern methods. The original plates to both GOBLETS I & II were destroyed years ago so these editions are reproduced from an original copy of each book supplied to us by Dr. Millard's daughter, Arlyne Millard Shortt. We felt the slight loss in detail of illustrations was more than accounted for by the textual and historical information supplied by the Millard books.

It is a tribute to Dr. Millard that his books are now used and enjoyed by a whole new generation of collectors.

DEDICATION

To Ruth Webb Lee, whose scholarly and pioneer work in the hitherto untrammeled field of American pressed glass, has not been excelled, and whose books have become the lexicon of dealers and collectors, and whose broad experience and acute vision has made her the last court of resort in expert and authoritative opinion on glass, I dedicate this little volume, with humble pride.

Diamond Thumbprint

Morning Glory

Plate 1

Barrel Thumbprint   Hotel Thumbprint   Washington   Mirror

Plate 2

Plain Smocking   Single Wedding Ring   Double Wedding Ring   Lined Smocking

Barrel Thumbprint—A heavy pattern of the 60's which shows much variation. Comes in clear only.

Hotel Thumbprint—A very large goblet of this pattern and made during the 60's. Clear only.

Washington—A heavy, flint goblet of the 60's and comes in clear only. There is a short stem of this same type.

Mirror—Another of the Argus variations and produced during the 60's. Clear only.

Plain Smocking—This pattern much resembles the honeycomb pattern but is much heavier, of flint glass with a good ring. A product of the 60's and comes clear only.

Single Wedding Ring—An attractive heavy goblet of the 70's and comes clear only.

Double Wedding Ring—A heavy goblet with evidence of lead glass make. Very good ring. Produced during the 60's and comes clear only.

Lined Smocking—Another of the smockings but with transverse lines through the bottom of the sulci. Product of the 60's. Clear only. There is also a pattern with knobbed stem.

Hair Pin, Plain—A rather light weight goblet with well defined loops at the top. A product of the 80's and comes in clear only.

Hercules' Pillar—A product of the 50's and is usually very crude, tall and ungainly. It is found in clear only.

Tall Argus—A heavy, flint glass goblet with a splendid ring. Produced during the 30's and is found in clear only.

Ribbed Palm — A product of the 60's and is found only in the clear.

Plate 3

Hair Pin, Plain   Hercules' Pillar   Tall Argus   Ribbed Palm

Plate 4

Bessimer Flute   Brooklyn Flute   Plain Tulip   Plain Mioton

Plate 5

Choked Ashburton   Proxy Ashburton   Giant Ashburton   Talisman Ashburton

Bessimer Flute—One of the many types of this pattern, made during the 60's and has a good ring and a clear, sparkling glass. Clear only.

Brooklyn Flute — Another heavy, flint glass goblet of the 60's and comes clear only.

Plain Tulip — A pattern produced during the 60's and is of heavy, ringing glass. Clear only.

Plain Mioton—A rather light goblet made during the 70's and comes clear only.

Choked Ashburton — A heavy, sparkling glass, goblet with a nice ring, produced during the 60's and comes clear only.

Proxy Ashburton—Another large and extremely heavy goblet of the 60's. Clear only.

Giant Ashburton—The largest goblet of this type to be found, measures nearly 4 inches across the top. Produced in the 60's and clear only.

Talisman Ashburton — A rather slender but heavy goblet of the same type. Made during the 60's and is found in clear only.

Barrel Ashburton—Another of the same type but considerably lighter in weight. Made during the 60's and comes in clear only.

Straight Banded Worchester — A heavy, tall goblet of the 60's and is distinctly different from the Ashburton family, having a band near the centre of the bowl and the loops opposite each other and not dodged as in the Ashburton. Clear only.

Slim Ashburton—A very narrowly constructed goblet of this well known pattern, made in the 60's and comes in clear only.

Flare Top, Belted, Worchester—A very heavy goblet with wide flare in the top. Made during the 60's and comes in clear only.

Plate 6

Barrel Ashburton   Straight Banded Worchester   Slim Ashburton   Flare Top, Belted, Worchester

Plate 7

| Galloway | Empire Colonial | Hinoto | Double Petal Tulip |

Plate 8

| Charleston | Square Flute | Conneticut Flute | Sexton Flute |

Galloway—A very pleasing, heavy goblet with large sparkling ovals. A product of the 70's and has been found only in clear.

Empire Colonial—A very heavy, flint glass goblet with a splendid ring. A product of the 40's and comes in clear and opaque white.

Hinoto—A very attractive goblet of fairly good weight and ring. Produced during the 70's and comes in clear only.

Double Petal Tulip—A heavy goblet of this type and showing the petals double or overlapping on the bowl. Made during the 50's and comes in clear only.

Charleston—A heavy goblet of the flute type but with 10 flutes and good knob stem, was produced during the 60's and is clear only.

Square Flute—As the name indicates the bowl is squarish and rather high with a splendid sparkle and ring. Produced during the 60's and comes in clear only.

Connecticut Flute—A rather tall and heavy goblet of this type without knob on stem and made during the 60's and comes clear only.

Sexton Flute—A very heavy, clear and sparkling goblet of the 60's and comes clear only.

Banded Vernon—A rather heavy goblet with honeycomb to near the top. Found in clear, light amber, blue, green and canary. A product of the 60's.

Giant Honeycomb—A very heavy goblet with good ring and honeycomb all over bowl to top and on stem to the foot. Clear only, and was made during the 50's.

Heavy New York—A pattern with design low on bowl but of heavy glass. Found in clear, amber, blue, green and canary. A product of the 70's.

Bumble Bee Honeycomb—A large, heavy goblet with knob stem. Found in clear only, and made during the 60's.

Plate 9

Banded Vernon   Giant Honeycomb   Heavy New York   Bumble Bee Honeycomb

Plate 10

Honeycomb Band   Lyston Honeycomb   Looped Band   Laredo Honeycomb
Honeycomb

Plate 11

Roman Key, Clear   Elk And Doe   Daisy And Button   Belted Worchester
Banded   With Amber Stripes   Knob Stem

Honeycomb Band—A rather heavy goblet with large barrel bowl and showing a honeycomb band around the bowl. Produced during the 80's. Clear only.

Lyston Honeycomb—A fairly light goblet with design low on the bowl, produced during the 80's and comes in clear, light amber, blue and canary.

Looped Band Honeycomb—Another goblet with the design low on the bowl and with transverse loops around the bowl. A product of the 80's and comes in clear only.

Laredo Honeycomb—A fairly heavy goblet with bold design and thick stem. Produced during the 70's and comes in clear, amber, blue, and canary.

Roman Key Clear, Banded—A pattern of this well known goblet with clear key but with two bands above and below the key. Made contemporary with others of this type. Clear only.

Elk And Doe—A pattern errioniously called Deer And Doe. A three panel goblet showing doe lying and buck running in one panel and standing in the other. A product of the 70's and clear only.

Daisy And Button—With Amber Stripes. One of the myriad pattern of this type, and is to be found clear, striped, amber, blue and canary.

Worchester Belted, Knob Stem—A goblet that has been classed with the Ashburtons, but is a distinctly different pattern. Made during the 50's and comes clear only.

Dickinson—A heavy goblet with a good ring, made during the 70's. Clear only.

Hawaiian Pineapple—Another heavy goblet and differing materially from the well known New England pineapple. Made during the 70's and comes in clear only.

Worchester, Creased—A pattern of the 50's and found in clear only.

Laminated Petals—A heavy goblet with good ring, produced during the 60's and clear only.

Plate 12

Dickinson   Hawaiian Pineapple   Creased Worchester   Laminated Petals

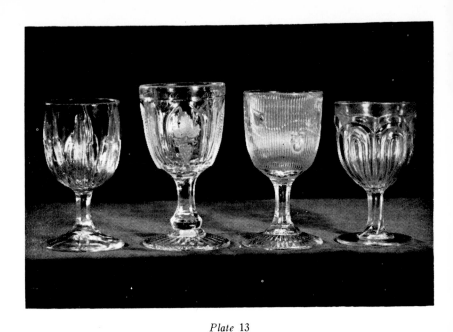

Plate 13

Stedman, Plain Base   Magnet And Grape   Bellflower, Fine Rib   Seneca Loop

Plate 14

Beaded Rosettes   Question Mark   Lotus   Balder

Stedman, Plain Base—Another of the group of this design produced during the 60's. Clear only.

Magnet And Grape—Frosted Leaf. A pattern of the 60's and clear only.

Bellflower, Fine Rib, Plain Stem, Rayed Base—Another variant of this family, produced during the 30's. Clear only.

Seneca Loop—A product of the 50's and is found in clear only.

Beaded Rosettes—A very attractive goblet of the 70's and is found in clear only.

Question Mark—Here is one of the many types of goblets produced during the 80's and is found in clear only.

Lotus—An unusually pretty goblet with finely stippled effect, often confused with Tree Of Life, and collectable in other pieces. It is a product of the 70's and comes in clear only.

Balder—A product of the 80's and was made in imitation of the cut glass so common in that period. Often shows gilt, red or purple on the top.

Dewdrop With Star—A pattern of the 70's and is found in clear only.

Horse, Cat And Rabbit—One of the animal goblets produced during the 70's and is found in clear only.

Bradford Grape—A heavy panelled grape pattern of the 70's and is found clear only.

Clear Fuchsia—A pattern of the 80's and is also found stippled.

Plate 15

Dewdrop With Star   Horse, Cat & Rabbit   Bradford Grape   Clear Fuchsia

Plate 16

Bellflower, Fine R'b   Bellflower, Coarse Rib   Ribbed Grape   Ribbed Ivy
Knob Stem, Barrel   Straight Sides   Clear Band
Shape

Plate 17

Rose In Snow   Stippled Roman Key   Swan   Clear Roman Key

Bellflower—Fine Rib, Knob Stem, Barrel Shape, plain base. Another of the patterns made during the 30's and is found in clear only.

Bellflower—Coarse Rib, Straight Sides, Rayed Base. A variation on the type of goblet found above and made during the same period.

Ribbed Grape—Clear Band. A pattern of the 50's and comes clear only.

Ribbed Ivy—A pattern of the 50's and is clear only.

Rose In Snow—A pattern of the 70's and comes in clear, amber, blue, canary, and milk white.

Stippled Roman Key—A pattern produced during the 80's and comes in clear only.

Swan—A product of the 70's and comes in clear, light amber, dark blue and canary.

Clear Roman Key—A pattern of this type showing a raised design on bowl. Clear only.

Jersey Swirl, Small—A pattern of the 80's and should show colors but no goblets have been found in colors.

Dahlia—A pattern of the 70's and is found in clear, amber, blue and canary. Colors are becoming rather expensive, especially amber and canary colors.

Cathedral—A pattern of the 80's and is to be had in clear, amber, blue, amethyst, and canary.

Hobnail With Fan Top—A pattern of the 70's and comes clear only.

Plate 18

Jersey Swirl, Small Dahlia Cathedral Hobnail With Fan Top

Plate 19

Krom   Barrel Excelsior   Giant Excelsior   Flare Top Excelsior

Plate 20

Hair Pin With   Pillar   Iconoclast   Three Bar Waffle
Thumbprint

Krom—A very heavy goblet with large stem, large almond shaped depressions and a heavy line thru each. It shows rough pontil on foot. Made during the 30's and comes in clear only.

Barrel Excelsior—A pattern of the 50's and comes in clear only.

Giant Excelsior — An extremely heavy goblet with solid diamonds at the cross bars. Made in 50's and clear only.

Flare Top Excelsior—A pattern of the 50's and made as indicated by name. Clear only.

Hair Pin With Thumbprint—A very heavy, flint glass goblet with a good ring and was produced during the 70's. It is found only in the clear.

Pillar—An excessively heavy goblet, with good ring, and often found rather crudely molded. A product of Bakewell, Pears & Co., of Pittsburg, Pa., during the 40's.

Iconoclast—A heavy goblet with fairly good ring, produced during the 70's. Clear only.

Three Bar Waffle—A product of the 80's and comes in clear only.

Barrel Huber—A heavy flint glass goblet of the 60's found only in clear.

Bigler—A pattern of the 50's which is heavy flint glass with a good ring. Clear only.

Grand Inverted Thumbprint — A goblet rather larger than the ordinary run of this pattern and has a squarish bowl with very large thumbprints. I have seen it in clear, amber, blue and canary.

Flaring Huber—A contemporary of the other Huber shown on this cut and of same age. Clear only.

Plate 21

Barrel Huber   Bigler   Grand Inverted   Flaring Huber
                              Thumbprint

Plate 22

Fedora Loop   New England Pineapple   Crystal   York Colonial

Plate 23

Teepee   Inverted Prism   Chain And Star Band   Flat Prisms

Fedora Loop—Knob Stem. A pattern of the 30's and comes in clear only.

New England Pineapple—A pattern produced during the 60's, very heavy and good ring. Clear only.

Crystal—A pattern of the 60's and clear only.

York Colonial—A pattern of the 40's and clear and opaque white.

Teepee—A goblet of the 80's and clear only.

Inverted Prism — A goblet very much on the order of the well known inverted thumbprint variety but with prisms on the inner side of the bowl. It is a late goblet, probably of the 90's and should show colors, but I have not seen them.

Chain And Star Band—A goblet of the late 70's or early 80's and found only in clear.

Flat Prisms—As the name indicates the prisms are flattened and makes a very sparkling appearance. Made in the 80's and comes clear only.

Prism And Clear Panels—A goblet showing three large clear panels and prisms between them, rather heavy and of good quality glass.

Jewel Band—A goblet of the 80's and clear only.

Bungalow — Another rather heavy goblet of the 80's with clear panels, clear only.

Three Stories—A goblet of the late 80's and very attractive. Clear only.

Plate 24

Prism & Clear Panels   Jewel Band   Bungalow   Three Stories

Plate 25

Windflower   Palmette   Princess Feather   Panelled Daisy

Plate 26

Oval Panel   Sawtooth, Plain Stem   English Hobnail
Panelled   Diamond Point
Plain Stem

Windflower—A pattern of the 80's, rather heavy, and found in clear only.

Palmette—A goblet produced in the 70's, clear only.

Princess Feather — Another goblet of the 70's and is found only in clear and milk white.

Panelled Daisy — A product of Bryce Brothers of Pittsburg, Pa., in the 70's and comes in clear and amber, the latter rare.

Oval Panel—A product of King Brothers, in the 80's and comes in clear, light amber, light blue, and canary.

Sawtooth, Plain Stem—A production of the 80's and comes in clear only.

English Hobnail Panelled—Made by Bryce Brothers in the 80's; comes in clear only.

Diamond Point — Plain Stem. A variation of the earlier diamond point, made in the 80's. Clear only.

Daisy And Block—A variant of the divers types of Daisy And Button. A pattern of the early 80's and collectable in clear only.

Radiant Daisy And Button—A product of the 80's and comes only in clear so far as I know.

Barred Daisy—A very attractive pattern which shows upright bars and diamond band. Produced in 80's and comes in clear only.

Tiawana—A goblet of late 80's and comes in clear only.

Plate 27

Daisy And Block   Radiant Daisy And   Barred Daisy   Tiawana
                              Button

Plate 28

Grape And Festoon   Finecut And Block   Jersey Swirl   Panelled Grape Band
With Shield

Plate 29

Philadelphia Centennial   Scarab   Liberty Bell   Pillar & Bull's Eye

Grape And Festoon With Shield— A goblet contemporary with the other patterns of this type, and is collectable in clear only.

*Finecut And Block—*A pattern of the 80's and is found with clear, amber, pink, blue, and deep canary colors on the blocks.

*Jersey Swirl, Buttermilk—*Another pattern of the 80's and comes only in clear.

*Panelled Grape Band—*A variation of the many grape patterns which were produced in the 80's and comes in clear only.

*Philadelphia Centennial—*A goblet produced just before the Centennial celebration and were produced by many glass factories. This is clear only.

*Scarab—*A heavy Sandwich glass piece, with good ring and sparkling glass, produced in the 60's. Clear only.

*Liberty Bell—*Rather light glass, produced in the middle 70's and clear only.

*Pillar And Bull's Eye—*One of the earliest makes of Bakewell, Pears & Co. Rather heavy and sparkling glass with a fair ring. Clear only. Period of 50's.

*Hearts Of Loch Laven—*A very elaborate and pretty goblet of the 80's, and comes clear only.

*Cut Log—*A fairly heavy, sparkling goblet of the late 70's. Clear only.

*Plume—*Another goblet of the 80's and a contemporary of the Feather. Clear only.

*Feather—*A product of the 80's and comes in clear only.

Plate 30

Hearts Of Loch Laven   Cut Log   Plume   Feather

Plate 31

Crackle Glass   Hops Band   Clematis   Fairfax Strawberry

Plate 32

Prism & Diamond Bars   Ladder   Diamond Medallions   Panelled Cane

Crackle Glass—This very thin glass is in a delicate peach blow color, and was produced in the 80's. If there are other colors I have not seen them.

Hops Band—A contemporary, in the 80's, of the many banded goblets where variation of the grape patterns were used. This one seems to indicate that it has not been misnamed by the collecting fraternity and so this name has been retained. It is clear only.

Clematis—A rather attractive· goblet because of its distinctly raised figures, is attributed to the 70's and comes in clear only.

Fairfax Strawberry — A very attractive pattern of this much used variety, with heavy figures on the lower portion of the bowl. A variety produced during the 80's. Clear only.

Prism And Diamond Bars—An attractive goblet with alternate heavy prisms and small diamonds in panels. Produced during the 80's. Clear only.

Ladder—Another of the same period as the former with alternate prism and ladder panels. Clear only.

Diamond Medallions—A very pretty goblet with raised diamonds, made in the 80's and is collectable in clear only.

Panelled Cane—Another goblet of the 80's and shows the characteristic cane panels alternating with the usual prisms. Clear only.

Stippled Fuchsia—A product of the 80's and comes in clear only.

Flattened Hobnail—A variation of the many types of glass produced during the 80's and comes clear only.

Printed Hobnail—Another goblet of the 80's and there should be colors with this pattern as clear and amethyst has been noted.

Panelled Hobnail—A rather scarce goblet that has been little known, was produced during the 70's and comes clear only.

Plate 33

Stippled Fuchsia   Flattened Hobnail   Printed Hobnail   Panelled Hobnail

Plate 34

| Panelled Daisy And Button | Bull's Eye With Fleur de Lis | Hobnail, Buttermilk | Daisy And Button With Oval Panels |

Plate 35

| Canadian | Maltese Cross | Medallion | Curtain Tie-Back |

Paneled Daisy And Button—A very pretty glass with its band and dividing pointed panels, which was produced during the 80's and comes in clear, dark amber, deep blue, green and canary.

Bull's Eye With Fleur de Lis—A very heavy goblet, with splendid ring and sparkling resiliance. It was produced during the 60's and is found in clear only.

Hobnail, Buttermilk—This massive Hobnail is shown here only that one might see what they are like, the swelled foot, continuous with the hobnailed stem, is outstanding. A product of an Ohio Glass factory during the 70's. Clear only.

Daisy And Button With Oval Panels—Another attractive type of the well known and often used pattern, shows three distinct and clear oval panels with alternate Daisy And Buttons. Produced during the 80's and comes in clear, dark amber, green, deep blue and canary.

Canadian—Where this piece was made has not been determined. The type of pattern and glass would indicate the 70's. Clear only.

Maltese Cross—This pattern is well named from its general design. It seems to be contemporary with the

Canadian. It comes only in clear.

Medallion—This pattern is also of the 70's and comes in the following colors, clear, amber, blue, green and canary.

Curtain Tie-Back—This is an old goblet, which from the weight of the glass and general appearance seems to be of the late 70's or early 80's. It is collectable in clear only.

Deer And Doe With Lily Of The Valley—This piece, with many others showing animals, birds, etc., are products of the 80's. It comes only in clear.

Owl And Possum—This, a very attractive goblet shows the owl on one side and the o'possom, lying low on a limb, on the other. The stem is frosted and represents the trunk of a tree. It is a product of the 80's. Collectable in clear.

Jumbo—This goblet was evidently named for P. T. Barnum's gigantic elephant, and was made in the 80's. The goblet has three divided panels with an elephant in different positions within each. It is very rare. Comes clear only.

Pigs And Corn—This is a goblet of the late 80's and is very much sought by collectors. It comes only in the clear.

Plate 36

Deer And Doe With   Owl And Possum   Jumbo   Pigs And Corn
Lily Of The Valley

Plate 37

Clear Ribbon   Cable   Frosted Ribbon   Harp

Plate 38

Stippled Star   Huber, Straight Sides   Star Rosetted   Twinkle Star

Clear Ribbon—This goblet is the type which shows the scalloped foot. It was made in the 80's.

Cable—A flint glass product of the 50's, with splendid ring. Comes only in clear in goblets.

Frosted Ribbon—A product of the late 70's or early 80's. Comes in clear only.

Harp—A heavy flint glass goblet, made in the 50's, with the design pressed into the flat surface on six sides. Comes only in clear.

Stippled Star—This is a Gillinger goblet made in the 70's, at Pittsburg, Pa. It comes in the clear only.

Huber, straight sides—This heavy flint glass goblet was made at Pittsburg, Pa., in the late 60's. It comes clear only.

Star Rosetted—Made in the early 80's and is found only in clear in goblets.

Twinkle Star—This is a clear goblet with a nice rounded knob at the foot and the surface has small five point stars on the inside. It seems to be a product of the late 80's. Comes in clear only.

Panelled Thumbprint—This heavy goblet is very attractive because of the alternate well-defined prisms of a coarse type and the rows of thumbprints. It is an early 80's pattern.

Honeycomb With Ovals—This, another variation of the New York and Vernon, was made by many glass factories from the 60's thru the 90's. I have only seen clear but it should show up in amber.

Mitered Dewdrop—An example of the 80's and a very attractive goblet. Comes in clear only.

Wahoo — This goblet shows the large ovals above the usual loops on the lower portion of the bowl. It was apparently made in the 70's. Clear.

Plate 39

Panelled Thumbprint   Honeycomb With Ovals   Mitered Dewdrop   Wahoo

Plate 40

Dodo   Gypsy   Diamond Splendor   Spear Point

Plate 41

Palm Stub   Loop With Fish Eye   Loop And Dart   Loop And Noose
                                     Diamond Ornaments

Dodo—A rather clumsily molded pattern, with the design low on the bowl. Glass rather heavy and probably of the 70's. Clear only.

Gypsy—Another goblet with design low on the bowl and rather crude. It is a goblet of the 80's. Clear only.

Diamond Splendor — A series of large, clear cut, diamonds, with deep cuts between, cover the bowl to a scalloped band near the top. A heavy glass of the late 70's. Clear.

Spear Point—A sparkling glass of medium weight made in the 80's. Comes in clear only.

Palm Stub—So called because of its close resemblance to a stunted palm. A product of the 80's and comes in clear only.

Loop With Fish Eye—This goblet, a variation of the loop & dart, was probably made at a later period, the early 80's. Clear only.

Loop And Dart With Diamond Ornaments—Is a production of Richards & Hotly, and was created in the late 60's. Comes clear only.

Loop And Noose—Another variation of the Loop & Dart patterns, is evidently of a later period. Comes in clear only.

Double Loop—There are no darts on the pattern therefore the Dart is left off the name. It is contemporary with the other loop & dart patterns of the 60's, and comes in clear only.

Loop And Dart With Round Ornaments—With its sister pattern was a product of the 60's and it also comes in clear only.

Double Leaf And Dart—This pattern, made in the early 70's follows closely after the general patterns of similar type. It is clear only. This pattern also shows stars in the band.

Loop & Dart—Was made in Pa., in the 60's and comes in clear only.

Plate 42

Double Loop   Loop And Dart With   Double Leaf And Dart   Loop And Dart
With Round Ornaments

Plate 43

Lily Of The Valley   Panelled Flowers   Bleeding Heart   Bleeding Heart
                                           Knob Stem   Plain Stem

Plate 44

New Pressed Leaf   Wild Fern   Garden Fern   Pressed Leaf

Lily Of The Valley—A goblet produced during the late 80's thru 90's. Comes clear only.

Paneled Flowers — A goblet produced during the 80's. Comes in clear only.

Bleeding Heart, Knob Stem—Design rather heavy and leaves well stippled. Made in 90's. Clear.

Bleeding Heart, Plain Stem—Here the design is rather low on the bowl and fainter, with a plain stem. It is also of the 90's. Clear only.

New Pressed Leaf—This is so designated to differentiate it from a similar pattern, each of which are a distinct pattern. This one has the wide leaves. A product of the 60's. Clear.

Wild Fern—Created in the 80's and comes in clear only.

Garden Fern—Another pattern of the 80's and shows more orderly arrangement of the fern fronds. Comes clear only.

Pressed Leaf—This pattern would indicate a possible later date than its predecessor. Leaves are sharply pointed and longer. Clear.

Bull's Eye And Spear Head—An attractive goblet fairly heavy and sparkling. Apparently of the 80's. Clear only.

York Herringbone—A variety of the well-known Herringbone, and a product of 80's. Clear only.

Spear Head—A very heavy goblet with design low on the bowl. Apparently of the 70's. Clear.

Cyclone—A product of the 90's and comes in clear only.

Plate 45

| Bull's Eye And Spear Head | York Herringbone | Spear Head | Cyclone |

Plate 46

Ruby Thumbprint, Clear   Pigmy   Sawtooth Band   Hawaiin Lei

Plate 47

Stippled Ivy   Beaded Ovals   Budded Ivy   Jewel With Dewdrops

Ruby Thumbprint, Clear—A goblet of the 90's and comes with clear top, red top, gilt top, and purple top.

Pigmy—Here is another banded goblet of the 80's and is found only in clear.

Sawtooth Band—Produced in the 80's and is found only in clear.

Hawaiian Lei—A goblet of the 80's and found only in clear.

Stippled Ivy—A product of the late 60's and comes in clear only.

Beaded Ovals—An attractive goblet with well balanced ovals surrounded by beaded bands. It is of the 80's and comes in clear only.

Budded Ivy—Another Ivy goblet of the late 60's and comes in clear only.

Jewel With Dewdrops — A fairly heavy goblet with beautiful proportions and bright glass. Appears to be of the 90's. Clear only.

Nail Head—A goblet of the 80's, that is only made in clear.

Oval Mitre—A fairly heavy goblet with design sunken into glass. Made in the 50's in Pa. Comes in clear only. Rather rare.

Paneled Jewels — A fairly heavy goblet with graduated beaded circles in panels. A product of the 80's. Comes in clear, amber, and blue.

Philadelphia—Made by New England Glass Co., in 60's. Comes in clear only.

Plate 48

Nail Head   Oval Mitre   Panelled Jewels   Philadelphia

Plate 49

Geddes   Aster Band   Peerless   Diamond Band

Plate 50

Mitered Frieze   Perkins   Ferris Wheel   Star And Crescent

Geddes—One of the myriad banded pattern goblets that came during the 70's. Rather heavy. Clear only.

Aster Band—Another odd goblet of early 80's and heavy. Clear only.

Peerless — A heavy goblet with pleasing design of diamonds, and knob stem. Was produced during the 60's. Clear only.

Diamond Band — A contemporary with Peerless and comes only in clear.

Mitered Frieze—A goblet belonging to the multiple Daisy & Button family. A product of the 80's. Clear only.

Perkins—A very elaborate pressed pattern of mixed figures, fairly heavy and good ring. Foot is rayed. Late 70's to early 90's. Clear.

Ferris Wheel — Another elaborate variant of the same family, but showing a definite wheel in the form of Daisies. Tall, sparkling glass and fairly good ring. Rayed and scalloped base. A product of late 80's to early 90's. Clear.

Star And Crescent — A beautiful, clear, sparkling goblet with elaboratee designs on bowl and looped knobs. Rayed base. Late 90's. Clear only.

Grape Band—A pattern of the 80's and clear only.

Festoon And Grape, Stippled Leaf —Made By Doyle Brothers of Pittsburg, Pa., during the 80's. Clear only.

Stippled Grape And Festoon, Stippled Leaf—Another pattern of the 80's and comes in clear only.

Arched Grape—Produced during the 80's, clear only.

Plate 51

| Grape Band | Festoon And Grape Stippled Leaf | Stippled Grape And Festoon, Stippled Leaf | Arched Grape |

Plate 52

Cabbage Rose   Open Rose. Heavy   Open Rose. Light   Falcon Strawberry

Plate 53

Snow Band   Two Panel   Wildflower   Willow Oak

Cabbage Rose—This pattern made in Virginia during the 60's and comes clear only.

Open Rose, Heavy—This is a pattern of the 70's and is found in clear only.

Open Rose, Light—Another of the same type but of lighter glass and a later production, the 80's clear only.

Falcon Strawberry—Another pattern of the 80's and comes in clear only.

Snow Band—This is a stippled band goblet of the 70's and comes in clear and amber.

Two Panel—A goblet of the 80's and comes in clear, amber, apple green, light yellowish green, blue and canary.

Wildflower—A pattern of the 70's and comes in clear, amber, blue, green and canary.

Willow Oak—A pattern made by Bryce Brothers of Pittsburg, Pa., in the 70's and is found in clear, amber, blue and canary.

Minerva—A product of the 70's and comes in clear only.

Odd Fellow—A goblet made in the 80's and is found in clear only.

Good-luck, Knob Stem—This goblet made in the 90's and is found in clear only.

Good-luck, Plain Stem — Another type made during the 90's and comes in clear only.

Plate 54

Minerva   Odd Fellow   Good-Luck, Knob Stem   Good-Luck, Plain Stem

Plate 55

Diamond Shield   Pillared Crystal   Staggered Prism   Scalloped Prism

Plate 56

Mitered Thumbprint   Loop And Argus   Maple Leaf, Clear   Georgia Belle

Diamond Shield—A goblet of the 80's and comes in clear only.

Pillared Crystal—A heavy sparkling goblet of the 70's and found in clear only.

Staggered Prism—A goblet belonging to the icicle family and made in the 80's. Clear only.

Scalloped Prism—A light goblet of the same type made in the 90's; clear only.

Mitered Thumbprint—A light goblet of the 90's and found in clear only.

Loop And Argus—Another light weight goblet of the 90's and comes clear only.

Maple Leaf, Clear—A pattern made in 70's on thru the 80's, showing rough stem in imitation of tree bark. It is found in clear, frosted, amber, green, blue and canary.

Georgia Belle—One of the heavy type of goblets made in imitation of cut glass and produced in the 80's thru the 90's; clear only.

Red Block—A goblet produced in the 90's and comes with clear top, red top and purple top.

Hickman—A heavy, peneled goblet of the 80's and is to be found in clear, amber and green.

Panelled Diamonds, Red Top — A goblet of the 80's that is found with both clear and red top.

Red Block And Fan—Another goblet of the 80's and is found with clear top and red top.

Plate 57

Red Block   Hickman   Panelled Diamonds,   Red Block And Fan
                                      Red Top

Plate 58

Cord Drapery   Hour Glass   Octagon Daisy &   Couchman
                                                  Button

Plate 59

Bartlett Pear   Barberry, Oval Berries   Currant   Barberry, Round
                                                                             Berries

Cord Drapery—A pattern of the 70's and comes in clear, amber, green and blue.

Hour Glass—A pattern of the 80's and is to be found in clear, amber and blue.

Octagon Daisy And Button—As the name indicates it has eight flat surfaces, rather good weight, and comes in clear, amber, blue, and canary.

Couchman—A heavy goblet of the pinwheel type made in the 70's and comes in clear, muddy amber, blue and green.

Bartlett Pear—One of the divers fruit patterns that were produced during the 80's. Clear only.

Barberry, Oval Berries—A product of the Fostoria, Ohio Glass Works, during the 70's. Clear only.

Currant—Another goblet of the 70's and clear only.

Barberry, Round Berries—A contemporary of the other pattern of this type, made in the 70's. Clear only.

Fruit Panels—A goblet showing three panels of differing fruits, made in 70's and clear only.

Rose Leaves—A goblet of the 80's and clear only.

Gandy Strawberry—A heavy type goblet with raised, and stippled figures on the bowl. Made in 70's and found only in clear.

Dunlop Strawberry—Another heavy goblet with large berries, rayed base and made in the 70's. Clear.

Plate 60

Fruit Panels   Rose Leaves   Gandy Strawberry   Dunlop Strawberry

Plate 61

Clear Stork   Frosted Stork   Flamingo   Scroll With Flowers

Plate 62

Owl In Horseshoes   Bouquet   Snake Skin And Dot   Silver Anniversary

Clear Stork—An attractive goblet produced during the 80's, clear only.

Frosted Stork—A goblet produced during early 70's and always frosted. It is becoming scarce.

Flamingo—A heavy attractive goblet of the early 80's and is found in clear only.

Scroll With Flowers—A product of the 80's and is found in clear and apple green but the latter is very scarce.

Owl In Horseshoes—A three panel goblet of the 80's and comes in clear only.

Bouquet—A rather heavy, flare top goblet of tthe 80's and is clear only.

Snake Skin And Dot — A pleasing squarish bowl, made during the 80's; clear only.

Silver Anniversary—A clear goblet with bands of silver overlay, made in the 80's. Clear only.

Prism With Loops—A goblet produced during the deluge of glass production, during the 80's. Clear only.

Prism And Bull's Eye—A goblet of the 70's, heavy and fairly sparkling, which was made in clear only.

Bull's Eye In Heart—A very elaborately designed pattern of the 70's and is to be found in clear, dark green and blue.

Tick-Tack-Toe—This goblet seems to be a product indigenous to Northern New York State, made during the 80's and is found in clear only.

Plate 63

Prism With Loops   Prism And Bull's Eye   Bull's Eye In Heart   Tick-Tack-Toe

Plate 64

Stippled Starflower   Orange Peel   Fan With Diamonds   Mountain Laurel
Banded

Plate 65

Milk White Strawberry   Opaque White   Opaque White   Cream Grape
            Honeycomb   Colonial

Stippled Starflower, Banded — A goblet of the 70's and is found in clear only.

Orange Peel—Another goblet of the 80's and is found in clear only.

Fan With Diamonds—A pattern of the 70's and comes in clear only.

Mountain Laurel—Another elaborate goblet, rather heavy, with much diamond point decoration, made in the 70's and is found in clear only.

Milk White Strawberry—A pattern of the 70's.

Opaque White Honeycomb—Another pattern of the 70's.

Opaque White Colonial — An extremely rare goblet of the 40's.

Cream Grape—A rather dignified goblet with bold figures, often showing brownish shading on the cream colored bowl. A product of the early white glass era.

Inverted Fern—A product of the 70's and comes in clear only.

Milk White Block And Fan—An attractive goblet of the 70's.

Milk White Fruit Panels—Another of the patterns produced during the milk glass period.

Pleat And Panel—A Bryce Brothers product of the 70's and this particular one has the large bars extending up into the clear band. There is another with the coarse bars ending at the plain band. Clear only.

Plate 66

| Inverted Fern | Milk White Block And Fan | Milk White Fruit Panels | Pleat And Panel |

Plate 67

Milton   Selby   Prism And   Panelled Sawtooth
                              Panelled Rosettes

Plate 68

Shovel   Crow-foot   Mitered Prisms   Mitered
                                    Diamond Points

Milton—One of the block type goblets that were so prevalent during the 80's. Is to be found in clear, amber and blue.

Selby—An attractive goblet with alternating clear sparkling panels and network. Made during the 80's and is clear only.

Prism And Panelled Rosettes — A very tall, flaring goblet with knob just above the foot. A product of the 80's and comes clear only.

Panelled Sawtooth—An attractive goblet of the late 70's and is found clear only.

Shovel—A three panel goblet of the 80's and comes only in clear.

Crow-foot—Another goblet of the 80's and clear only.

Mitered Prisms—An attractive goblet of the 80's and is found only in clear.

Mitered Diamond Points—A product of the 80's and is clear only.

Scottish Rite—A rather large goblet of thin glass, made in the 90's and comes clear only.

Needles And Pins—A goblet of the 80's and clear only.

My Lady's Work Box—A very large paneled goblet of rather thin glass, made during the 80's. Clear.

Wheat Sheaf — A goblet usually found with design rather shallow on the bowl. A product of the 70's and is found in clear only.

Plate 69

Scottish Rite   Needles And Pins   My Lady's Work Box   Wheat Sheaf

Plate 70

Portrait   Eastern Star   Dewdrop   New England
                                        With Inverted
                                        Thumbprint

Plate 71

Currant & Strawberry   Valencia Waffle   Gonterman   Stippled Medallion

Portrait—A rather attractive goblet showing three large ovals with a portrait of three differing figures, one in each panel. Clear only. 80's.

Eastern Star—A close copy of the Sandwich Star in so far as design is concerned, but with a clear band at top. Made during the 70's. Clear only.

Dewdrop With Inverted Thumbprint — A pattern of the 70's and is found in clear only.

New England—A three panel goblet showing pleasing scenes differing in each panel. Made in 70's. Clear.

Currant And Strawberry—A pattern produced during the 80's and comes in clear only.

Valencia Waffle—A rather large goblet with square foot, produced during 80's. Comes clear and amber, possibly blue.

Gonterman—A very attractive goblet with beaded panels on frosted field with an amber band at top and knob stem. Period of 80's.

Stippled Medallion—A goblet made in the 70's and comes in clear only.

Frosted Roman Key With Ribs—A product of the 60's and on thru 80's. Clear only.

Clear Polar Bear—A contemporary of the frosted one of the same type and is of the 80's.

Threaded—A rather heavy goblet of the 70's and comes clear only.

Stippled Band—A goblet difficult to find but not especially attractive. Made in the 70's, and is found only in clear.

Plate 72

Frosted Roman Key   Clear Polar Bear   Threaded   Stippled Band
With Ribs

Plate 73

Frosted Polar Bear   Prism & Diamond   Prism & Diamond   Popcorn
                          Point, Plain Stem   Point, Knob Stem

Plate 74

Frosted Flower Band   Jacob's Ladder   Sandwich Star   Classic

Frosted Polar Bear—One of the much- sought patterns and becoming scarce and high priced. It is an Ohio product and was made during the 80's. Comes frosted and clear.

Prism And Diamond Point, Plain Stem—This goblet is lighter than its compatriot, but is very attractive. It probably is of the 80's. Clear.

Prism And Diamond Points, Knob Stem—Is very heavy, with knob stem, neat bowl, brilliant and a good ring. A much earlier period than its predecessor and probably in 70's. Clear only.

Popcorn—A product of the late 60's and a very attractive goblet with rayed base. Clear only. Another type shows the ear of corn raised above the general surface.

Frosted Flower Band—A goblet of the 70's and becoming rather scarce and difficult to find. Stem and band are frosted. Clear only.

Jacob's Ladder—A very heavy goblet with good ring, brilliant and a nice facetted knob on stem. Made in 70's. Comes clear only.

Sandwich Star — Another very heavy and exceptionally brilliant pattern. Heavy facetted knob on stem. Bell ring. Made in 50's and is very scarce and hard to find. Clear only.

Classic — A beautiful goblet with frosted stem and panels. While made in the 80's commands a good price to own one of them. Clear only.

Fluted Icicle — An Icicle Variant and named from the bold flutes below on the bowl. A product of the 70's and comes in clear only.

Fine Rib, Plain Band—A pattern made during the 50's and is found in clear only. This type shows the plain band at the top.

Prism, Rayed Base—Another product of the late 50's and is found only in clear.

Amberino—A clear glass, of thin proportions, which rings like a bell. A pattern of the 80's. Clear only.

Plate 75

Fluted Icicle   Fine Rib, Plain Band   Prism, Rayed Base   Amberino

Plate 76

Coarse Rib   Short Ribs   Stedman. Barrel Shape.   Blaze
Rayed Base

Plate 77

Rose Sprig   Rosette   Dewdrop   Sunburst

Coarse Rib—A pattern of the 80's and comes clear only.

Short Ribs—Another of the prism type but with a clear band at top. Clear only. Made in 80's.

Stedman, Barrel Shape, Rayed Base —A pattern of the 60's and comes in clear only.

Blaze—A pattern of the 60's and comes clear only.

Rose Sprig—A pattern of the 80's and should be found in clear, amber, blue and canary but I have only found the clear.

Rosette—A very attractive goblet of the 70's and is found only in clear.

Dewdrop—A pattern begun in the 60's and continued for many years. It is to be found in clear, amber, blue and canary. Colors are difficult to find and are becoming rather dear in price.

Sunburst—Another pattern of the 70's and may be had in clear, amber and blue. Colors are rather hard to find.

Dew With Raindrop—A pattern very much sought and becoming scarce. Produced during the 80's. Clear only.

Tulip With Small Flowers — A rather heavy goblet produced during the 70's. Clear only.

Knotty Ash—This very attractive, flaring goblet with facetted knob stem, appears very much like a footed tumbler. It is a product of the 70's and may be had in clear and green.

Valentine—Is a product of the U. S. Glass Co., during the 70's and comes in clear only.

Plate 78

Dew With Raindrop   Tulip, Small Flowers   Knotty Ash   Valentine

Plate 79

Milk White
Lacy Dewdrop

Westward-Ho

Clear Ribbon
Round Foot

Beaded Grape

Plate 80

Waffle & Thumbprint
Bulb Stem

Frosted Actress

Tree Of Life

G. A. R.

Milk White Lacy Dewdrop — A product of the 70's and may be found in clear, blue, amber and white.

Westward-Ho—A Gillinder product of the 70's and is found in frosted only.

Clear Ribbon, Round Foot — A product of the 80's and is found only in clear.

Beaded Grape—A product of the period from 60's thru to 90's; this, one of the earlier patterns is excessively scarce. It may be had in clear and emerald green.

Waffle And Thumbprint, Bulb Stem—A product of the late 50's. Clear only.

Frosted Actress—A product of the 70's and is found clear also.

Tree Of Life—Another goblet of the 70's and found in two varieties, this one shows the letters P. G. Co., under foot. Frosted only.

G. A. R.—This rather tall and very heavy goblet was made as a souvenir to the National G.A.R. and this particular one was made for the meeting at Minneapolis, Minn., May, 1889. Clear only.

Square Waffle—A pattern of the 80's and clear only.

Waffle With Fan Top—Another pattern of the 80's and is found in clear only.

Lattice And Oval Panels — A product of the 70's, very heavy, and sparkling glass. Clear only.

Corcoran—A three panel goblet of the 80's and clear only.

Plate 81

Square Waffle   Waffle With Fan Top   Lattice & Oval Panels   Corcoran

Plate 82

IOI   Beaded Loop   Egyptian   Herringbone

Plate 83

Klondyke Strawberry   Holly   Beadle   Pittsburgh Centennial

IOI—A pattern of the 70's and is found in clear only.

Beaded Loop—A very attractive goblet made during the 90's and comes in clear only.

Egyptian—A pattern of the 70's and is found in clear only.

Herringbone — A product of the 80's and clear only.

Klondyke Strawberry—A pattern of the 70's with heavy design all over the bowl; clear only.

Holly—An attractive pattern of the 70's and becoming scarce. Clear only.

Beadle—A heavy goblet with oval paneled diamond points, clear only and made during 80's.

Pittsburgh Centennial — A rather light weight goblet created during the Centennial in the 70's, and is found clear only. The word "Centennial" is imprinted twice on the foot.

Ramsay Grape—A rather delicate design on bowl with ribbed band. Period of 80's and clear only.

Stippled Festoon And Grape, Clear Leaf—A product of Boyle Brothers of Pittsburg, Pa., during the 70's and is found in clear only.

Keystone Grape—A heavy grape goblet with brilliant keystones inserted in the design. Made during the 70's and clear only.

Grape With Thumbprint Band—Another pattern of the 70's, in which many of the later goblets show worn molds. Clear only.

Plate 84

Ramsay Grape   Stippled Festoon And   Keystone Grape   Grape With
                  Grape, Clear Leaf   Thumbprint Band

Plate 85

Beaded Grape Medallion

Beaded Grape Medallion, Banded

Beaded Acorn

Beaded Grape Medallion. Design on Foot

Plate 86

Late Panelled Grape

Scroll

For-get-me-not In Scroll

Baltimore Pear

Beaded Grape Medallion—A pattern of the 60's and is found clear only.

Beaded Grape Medallion, Banded—Another of the same period and type. Clear only.

Beaded Acorn—A pattern of the 70's and clear only.

Beaded Grape Medallion, Design On Foot—Made as a contemporary with the above patterns and comes in clear only. Each of the Beaded Grape Medallion goblets show an oval design, differing in each, on the foot.

Late Panelled Grape — A much sought goblet of the 90's and comes clear only.

Scroll—A pattern of the 70's and comes in clear only.

For-get-me-not In Scroll—A pattern, also, of the 70's and comes in clear only.

Baltimore Pear—A pattern while made during the 80's, is becoming scarce. Clear only.

Fish Scale—A product of Bryce Brothers of Pittsburg, Pa. During the 80's. Clear only.

Bull's Eye, Knob Stem—A very heavy goblet of the 60's and comes in clear only.

Panelled Diamonds And Flowers—Another heavy goblet of flint glass, made during the 70's and found in clear only.

Panelled Herringbone—A product of the 70's and is found in clear and emerald green. Heavier than the other Herringbone.

Plate 87

| Fish Scale | Bull's Eye Knob Stem | Panelled Diamonds & Flowers | Panelled Herringbone |

Plate 88

| Cannon Ball | Panelled "S" | Stedman
Straight Sided | Flame |

Plate 89

| Fine Cut And Panel | Panelled Diamonds | Diamond Cut With
Leaf | Loop With Dewdrops |

Cannon Ball—A very pretty and much sought goblet but of late production. Clear only.

Panelled "S"—A heavy goblet with a good ring, produced during the 70's and clear only.

Stedman, Straight Sided—Here is one of the varieties made during the 60's and is clear only.

Flame—A patterns belonging to the icicle type of goblet and produced during the 80's. It is found clear only.

Fine Cut And Panel—A goblet made during the 70's and is to be found in clear, amber, blue and canary.

Panelled Diamonds — A pattern of the 80's and is found in clear, amber, blue, amber stripes and canary.

Diamond Cut With Leaf—A product of the 70's and comes in clear and amber, but the latter is exceedingly scarce.

Loop With Dewdrops—A pattern of the 90's and comes clear only.

Romeo—A type of the myriad block patterns made during the 80's and is found clear only.

King's Curtain — A very attractive goblet of the 80's and is found clear only.

Fibber Block — A diamond block goblet made during the 80's. Clear only.

Pulaski Cube—A pattern of the 80's with knob stem and cubed to the top. Clear only.

Plate 90

Romeo   King's Curtain   Fibber Block   Pulaski Cube

Plate 91

Trellis   Beaded Oval Windows   Nokomis Swirl   English Hobnail
                                                                      Printed

Plate 92

Panelled Swirl   Short Teasel   Short Swirl   Granby

Trellis—Here is one of the ladder type of goblets that were made during the 80's. Clear only.

Beaded Oval Windows—A very attractive goblet of the 80's and is to be found in clear, amber, blue, green and amethyst.

Nokomis Swirl—Here is a late swirl but of attractive perspective and is to be found in clear, amber, blue and canary.

English Hobnail Printed — This is one of the myriad of patterns made during the 80's and comes only in clear.

Panelled Swirl—Another of the late swirl pattern, but with definite clear panels. Clear, amber and blue.

Short Teasel—By comparison this goblet is found with short teasel pattern, low on the bowl, and is of lighter construction. Period of 70's and clear only.

Short Swirl—Another late swirl of well defined prisms on the bowl. Clear only.

Granby—A rather heavy goblet with diamonds above and below and loops between them. Period of the 70's and is found in clear only.

Stippled For-get-me-not—This goblet, while made in the 80's, is much sought and is rather difficult to find. It is found in clear, amber and opaque white.

Roman Rosette — A pattern of the late 80's, but becoming difficult to find. Clear only.

Teardrop And Tassel—A pattern of the 70's and becoming scarce. Clear and cobalt blue, the latter being exceedingly scarce.

Lacy Dewdrop—A product of Duncan of Pittsburgh, Pa., during the 70's and is to be found in clear, amber, blue and milk white.

Plate 93

Stippled   Roman Rosette   Teardrop And Tassel   Lacy Dewdrop
For-get-me-not

Plate 94

| Heart | Frosted Circle | Bellflower, Fine Rib Banded | Arched Leaf |

Plate 95

| Owl In Fan | Florida Palm | Panelled Grape | Persian Spear |

Heart—A goblet of attractive outlines, made during the 70's and comes in clear only.

Frosted Circle—A goblet made during the 70's and is found also with clear circle.

Bellflower, Fine Rib, Rayed Base And Clear Band At Top—One of the rarer types of this pattern which were made from 30's thru 50's, and is found in clear, amber, sapphire blue and opaque white, but the colors are exceedingly scarce and hard to find.

Arched Leaf—A goblet of the 70's period and is found only in clear.

Owl In Fan—Another of the favorite type of birds, made in the 70's and comes in clear only.

Florida Palm—A rather heavy goblet of the fan palm type, produced during the 80's and is to be found in clear only.

Panelled Grape—It has been claimed that this pattern was produced in Indiana and while of the later period, the 80's, it is becoming difficult to find because it is so widely collected. It is found in clear only.

Persian Spear—A very heavy, clear and sparkling goblet of the 70's and comes clear only.

Block And Spear Point — A rather heavy and attractive goblet of the 80's and comes in clear only.

Waffle With Spear Points—Here is another attractive, heavy goblet with heavily rayed base and bulbuous stem. Period of 70's and is found only in the clear.

Portland—So named because of its having been produced at the Portland Glass Works. Period of the 70's and is clear only.

Honey Comb With Diamonds—Here is one of the wide variety of honeycomb patterns produced over a wide period of time and showing a variation in having diamonds between the honeycomb impressions. Clear only.

Plate 96

Block & Spear Point   Waffle With Spear Points   Portland   Honey Comb With Diamonds

Plate 97

Barley   Beaded Band   Lattice   Fleur de Lis

Plate 98

Powder And Shot   Magnet And Grape   Magnet And Grape   Stippled Chain
                    Stippled Leaf   Clear Leaf

Barley—A pattern made during the 70's and is to be found in clear only.

Beaded Band—Produced during the 70's and while it should show colors, I have not found them, if you do here is room for your notes.

Lattice — A rather attractive goblet of the 80's and comes in clear only.

Fleur de Lis—A rather heavy, clear glass of pleasing design raised above the surface. It is found in clear only in this design, but there are patterns showing stippled bowl with smaller flowers, that show colors.

Powder And Shot—A much sought goblet of the 70's and comes in clear only.

Magnet And Grape, Stippled Leaf— A product, evidently of the 80's and comes in clear only.

Magnet And Grape, Clear Leaf— A product, evidently of the 80's and comes in clear only.

Stippled Chain — Another stippled bowl goblet with festoon of chain on bowl, produced during the 70's and is found in clear only.

Purple Slag—A goblet that brings a good price and hard to get. Period of 80's. Barrel bowl.

Frosted Magnolia — A very attractive goblet of the 70's and is found only in frosted.

Spartan — Here is a goblet of the block type with well defined loops at the top, 70's and clear only.

Star In Bull's Eye—A rather heavy goblet of the 70's and is found in clear only.

Plate 99

Purple Slag   Frosted Magnolia   Spartan   Star In Bull's Eye

Plate 100

| Pinwheel | Prism & Diamond Band | Oval Two Panel | Flat Prisms |

Plate 101

| Pangyric | Circle And Dot | Job's Tears | Flying Robin |

Pinwheel—An attractive goblet with large pinwheels around bowl. A product of the 80's and is found in clear only.

Prism And Diamond Band — A heavy goblet with prism top and well defined diamonds forming a band on lower part of bowl. A product of the 70's and clear only.

Oval Two Panel — A large, rather thin, goblet of sparkling glass, with large panels on bowl. A product of the 80's and comes in clear only.

Flat Prisms — Here is one of the many goblets in the prism type of design. This one, rather light in weight, shows a series of flattened prisms below a plain band at the top. A product of the 80's and clear only.

Pangyric—A heavy goblet with unusually attractive design, showing upright and transverse bars with crescents and small bull's eyes. It has a heavy knobbed stem. A product of the 70's and clear only.

Circle And Dot—A medium weight goblet with attractive design on bowl,

with plain round knobbed stem. A product of the 80's and has been found only in the clear.

Job's Tears—A medium weight goblet with series of elongated tear-drops covering the bowl and a rather heavy knob stem. Made during the 80's and has been seen in clear only.

Flying Robin—A fairly heavy goblet with fluted bowl below and panels showing birds in flight. A product of the 70's and clear only.

Scroll And Dots—A very expressive goblet of medium weight and attractive design. Made during the 80's and has only been seen in clear.

Churchill—A fairly heavy goblet of the 70's and comes in clear only.

Double Beetle Band — A medium weight goblet of the 80 period and comes in clear only.

Banded Icicle — One of the many types of the familiar icicle, but in this case with fine lines around base of bowl. A product of the 80's and comes in clear only.

Plate 102

Scroll And Dots   Churchill   Double Beetle Band   Banded Icicle

Plate 103

| Rabbit Tracks | Roman Key
With Loops | Squirrel | Martha's Tears |

Plate 104

| Diamond Block | Two Panel Waffle | Square Panes | Shamrock |

Rabbit Tracks—A light weight goblet of the 80's and comes in clear only.

Roman Key With Loops—A heavy goblet of very clear, sparkling glass and good ring. In this case the Roman key is cut deeply into the bowl and forms a very attractive and pleasing aspect. A product of the 70's. Clear only.

Squirrel—A splendid example of the animal goblets made thru the 70's and 80's. This goblet is becoming scarce and commands a good price. It is found in clear only.

Martha's Tears—A rather light goblet with pretty tear drops on lower aspect of the bowl, and was made during the 80's. Clear only.

Diamond Block—A square type bowl of heavy construction, and with the blocks in large diamonds covering bowl, product of the 80's and has been found only in clear.

Two Panel Waffle — One of the many types of this design, but having the panels cut into equal parts by bars; nice knob stem. A pattern of the 80's and has been seen in clear only.

Square Panes—A fairly heavy goblet with 4 large clear panes divided by prisms and showing very sparkling glass. A product of the 80's and clear only.

Shamrock—A medium weight goblet showing a cluster of three shamrocks in each of three panels. A product of the 80's and clear only.

Colossus—A rather large goblet of light weight and with pleasing design on the bowl. A product of the 80's and clear only.

Zipper—As the name indicates the bright prism bars are connected with a modern zipper. Rather heavy and sparkling glass. Ring knob at the foot. Made during the 80's and clear only.

Spalding — A rather tall, slender goblet with design low on the bowl. Made during the 80's and has been seen in clear only.

Block And Jewel—One of the many goblets with a block type of design. Made during the 80's and has been seen in clear only.

Plate 105

Colossus   Zipper   Spalding   Block And Jewel

Plate 106

Panelled Wild Daisy   Broken Column   Columbus Coin   Coachman's Cape

Plate 107

Balloon   Lined Stars   Catawba Grape Band   Hobnail, Plain Stem

Panelled Wild Daisy—A rather thin and light weight goblet of the 80's and clear only.

Prism And Broken Column — A medium weight goblet with pretty sparkling prisms broken by a cross bar. Made during the 80's and clear only.

Columbus Coin — One of the many souvenirs of the Chicago, Ill., World's Fair. Becoming scarce and most coin glass demands a good price. A product of the early 90's. Clear only.

Coachman's Cape — A light weight goblet made during the 80's and is found in clear only.

Balloon—A large, thin goblet with double bulging effect of the bowl and pretty prism design. A product of the 80's and clear only.

Lined Stars—A product of the 90's and a very pleasing expression of the star design. The bowl is stippled and the stars are clear and flat. Clear only.

Catawba Grape Band — Another of the many grape patterns so rife in the 80's and comes in clear only.

Hobnail, Plain Stem—One of the attractive goblets from an ever searched for pattern. A product of the 70's and is to be found in clear, amber and blue. Note also, elsewhere, the large buttermilk type.

Loop And Moose Eye — A heavy goblet of the 70's and of very attractive design. Clear only.

Lightning — A rather expressive type of small goblet with zigzag bars on bowl. A product of the 80's and clear only.

Art — A very heavy goblet of an extremely pretty design, alternating large tear drops and heavy diamonds. A product of the 60's and is found only in clear.

Fretted Vault—A light goblet with a series of overlapping cathedral points. Produced in the 80's and is found in clear only.

Plate 108

Loop And Moose Eye   Lightning   Art   Fretted Vault

Plate 109

Bull's Eye And   Clear Circle   Belt Buckle   Moon And Star
Diamond Panels

Plate 110

Banded Buckle   Buckle With Star   Buckle   Fine Cut

Bull's Eye And Diamond Panels—A goblet of the buckle family, has alternating clear panels and diamond points. Of the late 70's. Clear only.

Clear Circle—A modification of the well known frosted circle. Probably in the 80's. Clear only.

Belt Buckle—Made in the 80's and is found in clear only.

Moon And Star, Clear—A variation of the frosted moon and star and probably of the early 90's. Comes in clear only.

Banded Buckle—A Gillinder product and made in the late 60's. Clear only.

Buckle And Star — A variation of the buckle and was created by Bryce Brothers in the 80's. Clear.

Buckle—A goblet produced in late 60's and is found in clear only.

Fine Cut—A very attractive goblet produced by Bryce Brothers in the 70's. Comes in clear, canary, blue and probably amber.

Panelled English Hobnail With Prisms — A rather large and heavy goblet of the 80's and comes clear and with variable tops in gilt, etc.

Flying Birds—A fairly heavy goblet with flocks of birds in flight and a reeded stem. Produced during the 70's and clear only.

Cord Rosette—An attractive goblet with the design created by the use of the cord entirely. A product of the 80's and clear only.

Shrine—A typical star and crescent type of goblet with a very pleasing design. Made during the 80's and clear only.

Plate 111

Panelled English Flying Birds Cord Rosette   Shrine
Hobnail With Prisms

Plate 112

LaClede   Clear Diagonal Band   Wheat And Barley   Panelled Ivy

Plate 113

Lace   Double Wedding Ring   Block And Circle   Interlocking Crescents
Heavy

LaClede — A rather heavy goblet of the period in which many were made imitating cut glass. This is a very attractive goblet and is found in clear, dark amber and green.

Clear Diagonal Band—A product of the 80's and is found in clear only.

Wheat And Barley — A product of the 70's and is collectable in clear, amber, blue and canary.

Panelled Ivy — A pattern bearing close resemblance to. the familiar panelled for-get-me-not, and produced during the 80's. Clear only.

Lace—A rather light weight goblet, but of striking design. Produced in the 80's. Clear.

Double Wedding Ring, Heavy — A very heavy goblet with fairly good ring and rather dull glass often greasy and dull in appearance. 60's and clear.

A heavier pattern than the one listed elsewhere.

Block And Circle—A pretty goblet with a double knobbed stem and fairly heavy. Good ring. Made in 60's and comes in clear only.

Interlocking Crescents — A heavy goblet with a nice lobulated knob stem. Product of the 70's. Clear.

Loganberry And Grape — A goblet produced in the 90's and clear only.

Acorn — A very attractive goblet with bold design on the bowl. Of the 70's. Clear only.

Cherry — A Pittsburgh pattern of the 70's and comes in clear and opaque white.

Frosted Leaf—A product of the 60's and becoming rather expensive to obtain. Clear only.

Plate 114

Loganberry & Grape   Acorn   Cherry   Frosted Leaf

Plate 115

Duke   Ribbon, Bulging Sides   Ribbon, Straight Sides   Frazier

Plate 116

Clover And Daisy   Holly Leaves   Rose Of Sharon   Sugar Pear

Duke — One of the myriad forms produced during the 80's and comes clear only.

Ribbon, Slightly Bulging Sides—A much sought pattern and bringing fairly good prices now and becoming scarcer. Produced during the 50's and no colors were made.

Ribbon, Straight Sides—A contemporary with the last named and slightly taller and sides straight.

Frazier—One of those goblets made in imitation of cut glass and produced during the 80's and 90's. Clear only, but with red top.

Clover And Daisy — A pattern of the 80's and is found only in clear.

Holly Leaves — Another pattern of the 80's and clear only.

Rose Of Sharon — A large, single rose, produced during the 70's and is found clear only.

Sugar Pear—One of the myriad of fruit patterns, produced during the 80's and is clear only.

Hamilton With Leaf—A heavy goblet, rather dull appearance of the glass. A product of late 70's and comes in clear only.

Block And Thumbprint With Knob Stem—A Gillinder product of the 50's, heavy with facetted knob stem. Comes in clear only.

New England Centennial—A heavy, brilliant goblet with a good ring, clear prismed on a very tall straight bowl, with spread eagle and stars on one side while on the other is the word, "Centennial," surrounded by stars. Product of the 80's and clear only is found.

Hamilton — A product of the 70's and a very desirable pattern. Both Hamiltons are becoming scarce and hard to find. Clear only.

Plate 117

Hamilton With Leaf   Block & Thumbprint   New England   Hamilton
Knob Stem   Centennial

Plate 118

Lincoln Drape   Horn Of Plenty   Tulip With Sawtooth   Lincoln Drape

Plate 119

Beaded Oval   Deer And Pine Tree   Ashman   Beaded Dewdrop
And Scroll

Lincoln Drape With Tassel — A heavy goblet with a good ring. Produced shortly after the death of President Lincoln in the 60's. Clear only.

Horn Of Plenty — A Sandwich product of the 50's, very heavy, brilliant and with good ring. Nice facetted knob stem. Clear only.

Tulip With Saw Tooth — A very heavy, tall goblet with good sparkle and ring. Facetted knob stem and product of Bryce Brothers of Pittsburgh, Pa., during the 60's. Clear only.

Lincoln Drape—A contemporary of the one above and made in the 60's. Comes in clear only.

Beaded Oval And Scroll—A goblet produced in Pennsylvania during the 80's. Clear only.

Deer And Pine Tree—A very tall goblet with the design on each of two sides, created in late 70's. There may be colors in goblets, but they have not shown up yet.

Ashman—A large, showy goblet of the squarish type and square foot, with square creased knob stem, alternate clear panels which often are etched. A product of the 80's. Clear and amber.

Beaded Dewdrop — An attractive panelled goblet of the 80's. Comes in clear only.

Hand — A product of the O'Hara Glass Company of Pittsburgh, Pa., during the 80's. A very attractive goblet that is hard to find. Clear.

Darling Grape—A very tall, slender goblet with large clusters of grapes on bowl and a scalloped foot with the same design on the foot. Produced during the 80's. Clear only.

Anheuser-Busch "Faust"—An Anheuser-Busch goblet that was used to advertise their ale. Becoming scarce and hard to find. Made in 80's. Clear only.

Anheuser-Busch "A"—A tall, slender ale goblet, with design raised on surface as in the case of the one above it. Made in 80's. Comes in clear only.

Hand   Darling Grape   *Plate* 120   Anheuser-Busch   Anheuser-Busch "A"
                                                          "Faust"

Plate 121

Girl And Fan   Actress   Psyche And Cupid   Cupid And Venus

Plate 122

Cane   Stars And Bars   Bee Hive   Panelled For-get-me-not

Girl And Fan—A rather heavy goblet with pleasing design. A product of the 80's. Clear.

Actress—Another heavy goblet and pleasant to look upon. Two opposing medallions with lady in different poses. Product of 80's. Clear only.

Psyche And Cupid—A goblet of the late 70's and is found only in clear.

Cupid And Venus—This a product of Richards & Hartley of Terentum, Pa., and was made in the late 70's. It is found in clear only.

Cane — A goblet made in the 80's, and comes in the following colors—Clear, amber, canary, blue and apple green.

Stars And Bars—A product of the early 80's and comes in clear only.

Bee Hive—A very attractive, sparkling goblet produced in the late 80's. Clear only.

Panelled For-get-me-not—A goblet of the late 70's and produced on a type of bowl used for other patterns. It comes in clear, golden amber, blue, apple green and amethyst.

Panelled Dewdrop — A pattern of the late 70's and showing dewdrops on the foot of one while the other is plain. Collectable in clear only.

Diamond Point, Knob Stem — A heavy, flint glass goblet with good ring, produced from the 50's through several decades. Clear only.

Sawtooth, Knob Stem—This goblet probably dates a beginning in the 50's and was made by many glass factories through many years. It comes only in clear.

Panelled Diamond Point—A goblet produced in the 60's and comes in clear, deep blue, canary and amber.

Plate 123

Panelled Dewdrop   Diamond Point   Sawtooth, Knob Stem   Panelled
                     Knob Stem   Diamond Point

Plate 124

Beaded Tulip   Teasel   Kallbach   Thistle Shield

Plate 125

Brilliant   Eugenie   Waffle & Thumbprint
Knob Stem   Gothic

Beaded Tulip—This is an Ohio production of the 70's and comes clear only.

Teasel—This goblet was made by Bryce Brothers of Pittsburgh, Pa., and is a product of the 70's. Comes clear only.

Kallbach—A very heavy, odd goblet of the 70's and comes in clear only.

Thistle Shield—A rather attractive goblet of the 80's and comes in clear only.

Brilliant — Here is a very heavy, brilliant goblet with good ring and a rayed base, that was made during the 70's. It is clear only.

Eugenie — Here is another of the heavy type goblets of the 50's, and made in Pittsburgh, Pa. It is collectable in clear only.

Waffle And Thumbprint, Facetted Knob Stem — A beautiful, brilliant goblet of the late 60's, rather tall and with good ring. It is found in clear only.

Gothic—A heavy goblet of the 60's and is found in clear only.

Sprig—A rather light weight goblet, but of brilliant glass, was made in late 80's and can be found in the clear.

Chilson—Here is a very heavy and beautiful goblet with the characteristic loops below on the bowl and alternating large bull's eyes and large rosettes. It comes in clear only. 50's.

Prism And Flute—This rather heavy goblet with a fairly good ring, shows the flutes below on the bowl with a narrow prism band above them, is a product of the 70's and is found in clear only.

Block And Thumbprint—A pattern made at a later period than the others of this type, probably in the 80's, and with a rather wide, clear band at the top. Clear only.

Plate 126

Sprig   Chilson   Prism And Flute   Block & Thumbprint

Plate 127

Cord And Tassel　　　　Plaid　　　　Basket Weave　　　　Sheraton

Plate 128

Sheaf And Diamond　　　Mikado Fan　　　Prism & Daisy Bar　　　Currier & Ives

Cord And Tassel—A product of the 70's which is collectable in clear only.

Plaid — Here is a heavy goblet of the basket-weave type, but of older manufacture. Rather heavy with heavy weave in raised effect. It is found only in clear.

Basket Weave — A pattern of the 70's and is found in clear, amber, blue, canary and milk white.

Sheraton — A goblet found to be very common in Pennsylvania, and was created apparently in the 80's. It comes in clear, amber and blue.

Sheaf And Diamonds—A pattern of the 80's, which is found in clear only.

Mikado Fan—Another brilliant goblet of the same period and found in clear only.

Prism And Daisy Bar — Here is a pretty goblet with definitely refractive

bars alternated with amber stripes of the daisy type. A product of the 80's and may show other colored stripes.

Currier & Ives — A product of the late 60's, which comes in clear and blue.

Chestnut — A goblet with a heavy design on the bowl, made during the 80's and comes in clear, amber and blue.

Daisy And Button With Thumbprint—A much desired design of this pattern and is found in clear, amber, blue and canary.

Daisy And Button With Cross Bar And Thumbprint Band—A contemporary of the above pattern and found in clear, dark amber, light amber, blue and canary.

Jeter Daisy And Button—A pattern showing the design extended onto the foot. It has been seen only in clear.

Plate 129

Chestnut   Daisy And Button With Thumbprint   Daisy And Button With Cross Bar & Thumbprint Band   Jeter Daisy & Button

Plate 130

Arab   Dewdrop In Points   Double Ribbon   Marquisette

Plate 131

Moose Eye In Sand   Brooklyn   Diamonds And Thumbprint   Diamond, Thumbprint With Square Base

Arab — A goblet made in the 70's and comes only in clear.

Dewdrop In Points—Another goblet of the stippled type and probably contemporary with the Arab. Found in clear only.

Double Ribbon — This is the type that shows the double frosted ribbons to one clear, is of lighter material than the frosted ribbon and is of the 80's. Clear only.

Marquisette –A pattern made in the 70's and comes in clear only.

Moose Eye In Sand—Another stippled bowl goblet with large ovals clear and with beaded edge. Produced during the 80's. Clear only.

Brooklyn — Here is a heavy, flint glass goblet with good ring. A product of the 70's and is found in clear.

Diamonds And Thumbprint — Another fairly heavy goblet with a band of diamonds around the bowl and thumbprints above. Clear only.

Diamond, Thumbprint With Square Base—Here is one of those cheap goblets that were offered as a premium with merchandise. A product of the 80's and may be had in full sets. Clear only.

Panelled Cherry—A product of the 80's and is found only in the clear.

Thistle—A pattern of the 70's and should not be confused with the panelled thistle. Comes in clear only.

Messercau Blackberry — A pattern of the 70's and comes clear only.

Gooseberry—Another pattern of the 70's and generally shows the design rather weakly impressed on the bowl. Clear and milk white.

Plate 132

Panelled Cherry   Thistle   Messereau Blackberry   Gooseberry

Plate 133

Block House   Garfield Drape   Drapery   Three Panel

Plate 134

Frosted Circle   Mioton, Knob Stem   Hexagon Flute   Thousand Eye

Block House—A rather heavy goblet that was made during the 70's and comes in clear and dark amber.

Garfield Drape—A product of 80's and is found only in clear.

Drapery—A product of the 70's and is found only in the clear.

Three Panel — Made at Tarentum, Pa., during the 70's and comes in clear, light amber, dark amber, blue and canary.

Frosted Circle — This rather heavy goblet comes with the circle clear and frosted, and was produced during the 70's. Clear and frosted.

Mioton, Knob Stem — This heavy, flint glass goblet is of the fluted type with a large knob stem and good ring. Produced during the 60's.

Hexagon Flute — Here a rather heavy goblet with six large flutes and a hexagon foot. Produced during the 70's and is clear only.

Thousand Eye — An attractive and much sought pattern that was produced during the 70's, and is collectable in clear, light amber, dark amber, apple green, blue and canary.

Banded Cube—A cube with a plain band at the top and with large knob stem. Made during the period of 70's thru 80's. Clear only.

Cube—Probably the oldest of this type goblet, and is found in clear only.

Cube With Square Stem—A variety of the 80's and comes clear only.

Block And Fan—Another goblet of the 80's and is found with red top.

Plate 135

Banded Cube   Cube   Cube, Square Stem   Block And Fan

Plate 136

Block With   Diamond Block   Hexagon Block   Block & Double Bar
Sawtooth Band   With Fans

Plate 137

Tandem Bicycle   Columbian Exposition   Snake Drape   Ionia

Block With Sawtooth Band — A goblet of the 80's and comes clear only.

Diamond Block With Fans — Another of the 80's and comes clear only.

Hexagon Block—A goblet produced during the 80's and is to be found only in the clear.

Block And Double Bar — A goblet made during the 90's and clear only, often etched.

Tandem Bicycle—An attractive goblet of the 90's and clear only.

Columbian Exposition — A goblet created during the late 80's and is found clear only.

Snake Drape—A rather heavy goblet of the late 70's or early 80's and clear only.

Ionia — A product of the 80's and clear only.

Jewelled Drapery—Made during the 80's and is to be found in clear only.

Dahlia And Festoon — A rather heavy goblet with completely stippled field and bold design. Made during the 80's and clear only.

Dewdrop Band — A product of the 70's and is found only in clear.

Primrose — A product of the 70's and is to be found in clear, amber, blue, green and canary.

Plate 138

Jewelled Drapery   Dahlia And Festoon   Dewdrop Band   Primrose

Plate 139

Star, Flower Band   Broken Column   Stippled Peppers   Inverted Loops And Fans

Plate 140

Barred   Butterfly And Fan   Diagonal Band   Enigma
For-get-me-not   And Fan

Star Flower Band—A pattern of the 80's and is found only clear.

Broken Column—A heavy goblet of the 70's and very brilliant. Clear only.

Stippled Peppers — A patter of the 80's and is found in claer only.

Inverted Loops And Fans—A pattern of the 80's and clear only.

Barred For-get-me-not — A pattern of the 70's and is to be found in clear, golden amber, blue, apple green and canary.

Butterfly And Fan — A pattern of the 70's and is found in clear only.

Diagonal Band And Fan—A pattern of the 80's and is found clear only.

Enigma—A rather attractive goblet of the scroll and herringbone type, made during the 80's and comes in clear only.

Egg In Sand—An attractive goblet with the design raised above the surface. A product of the 70's and comes in clear, amber and blue.

Beaded Frog's Eye — A pattern of the 80's showing stippled bowl with clear ovals and beaded band around them. Clear only.

Cat 'O Nine Tails And Ferns—This is another of the patterns made during the 80's and comes in clear only.

Priscilla—A widely flared top and rayed base. Period of the 80's. Clear only.

Plate 141

Egg In Sand   Beaded Frog's Eye   Cat 'O Nine Tails And Ferns   Priscilla

Plate 142

Kokomo   Viking   Daisy And Button   Panelled Daisy And
                                  With Almond Band   Button With Flat Stem

Plate 143

Shield And Anchor   Lee   Shell And Tassel   Frosted Roman Key
                                                   With Flutes

Kokomo — A pattern made during the late 80's and comes clear and with red top.

Viking — A very attractive lattice type goblet with fan bursts near top, rather heavy and a clear, sparkling glass. Clear only.

Daisy And Button With Almond Band—A very acceptable type of this much sought pattern, which was produced during the 80's and should show the usual colors of that pattern.

Panelled Daisy And Button With Flat Stem — A type of this pattern made during the 1900's, and is only shown here as a variant of that pattern. I have only seen it in the clear.

Shield And Anchor—A product of the 80's and comes only in clear.

Lee—A very heavy, sparkling goblet. Named for Ruth Webb Lee, and made during the 70's. Clear only.

Shell And Tassel—A product of the Portland Glass Co., during the 70's, and comes with knob and plain stem.

Frosted Roman Key With Flutes— A product of the 60's. Comes clear and frosted.

Thayer — A very clear, sparkling goblet of the 80's and comes in clear only.

Gormand Inverted Thumbprint — A product of the 80's and comes in clear, amber, blue, green and canary.

Straight Sided Slag—A goblet becoming scarce and demands good prices to own.

Milk White Ivy In Snow — A pattern of the 60's and hard to find.

Plate 144

Thayer   Gormand Inverted   Straight Sided Slag   Milk White
                   Thumbprint   Ivy In Snow

Plate 145

Crystal Wedding   Panelled English   Bohemian Red   Sqeustered Crystal
                     Hobnail, Red Top

Plate 146

Ivy In Snow,   Milk White   Thumbprint And   Shields
Red Leaves   Blackberry   Panelled Swirl

Crystal Wedding — A cobalt blue goblet with pleasing design low on the bowl, this is found in the clear and cobalt blue and should show the amber also, but I have not seen it.

Panelled English Hobnail With Red Top—This is a pattern of the 80's and comes both clear, red top and perhaps gilt top.

Bohemian Red, Vintage Pattern—A goblet of the 70's and blown. Is very thin with a good ring.

Sqeustered Crystal—This is one of those goblets with enamel attached and belongs to the type of the 90's. Clear only.

Ivy In Snow, Red Leaves—A product of the 60's and comes clear, amber, blue, milk white and with red leaves and berries. Very rare.

Milk White Blackberry—A product of the 70's and is found in clear also.

Thumbprint And Panelled Swirl— A goblet of the 70's and is found in clear only.

Shields — A pattern created during the 80's and is found in clear only.

Hamilton With Frosted Leaf — A product of the 70's and comes clear, frosted and without leaf.

Flack—A heavy goblet of the 70's and with intricate design. Clear only.

Eureka—A product of the 60's and comes in clear only.

Magnet And Grape, Frosted, With Tendrils On Grape Bunch—A goblet made during the 70's and is found only in the clear.

Plate 147

| Hamilton With Frosted Leaf | Flack | Eureka | Magnet And Grape Frosted, Tendrils On Grape Bunch |

Plate 148

Manting   Fine Rib To Top   Ribbed Grape To Top   Festoon And Grape
                                                                      With Veined Leaves

Plate 149

Baby Face   Three Face   Frosted Lion   Frosted Festal Ball

Manting—A rather heavy goblet of the 70's and comes clear only.

Fine Rib To Top—A pattern of the 70's and comes in clear only.

Ribbed Grape To Top—A goblet of the 50's and comes clear only.

Festoon And Grape With Veined Leaves — A product of the 80's and comes in clear only.

Baby Face—A goblet produced during the 70's and comes in clear only.

Three Face—Another pattern of the 70's and comes in clear only.

Frosted Lion—A pattern of the 70's and is found in clear only.

Frosted Festal Ball — A pattern of the 80's and is found in clear only.

Grant And Wilson — A product of the 80's and is found in clear only.

Pecorah—A pattern of the 80's and comes in clear only.

Amulet — Another pattern of the 80's and is found only in clear.

Blucher—A goblet produced during the 80's and comes in clear only.

Plate 150

Grant And Wilson   Pecorah   Amulet   Blucher

Plate 151

| Stanley Inverted Thumbprint | Waterford Inverted Thumbprint | Diamond Quilted | Orion Inverted Thumbprint |

Plate 152

| Daisy And Button With Clear Lily | Panelled Heather | Water Lily | Bismarc Star |

Stanley Inverted Thumbprint — A product of the 80's and comes in clear, amber, blue, green and canary.

Waterford Inverted Thumbprint—A product of the 80's and comes in clear, amber, blue, green and canary.

Diamond Quilted — A goblet produced during the 80's and is found in clear, light amber, dark amber, canary, pale amethyst, dark amethyst, light blue, periwinkle blue and apple green.

Orion Inverted Thumbprine — A product of the 80's and nas been seen in clear only.

Daisy And Button With Clear Lily —A pattern of the 80's and comes in clear only.

Panelled Heather — A goblet produced during the 80's and is found in clear only.

Water Lily — An attractive goblet of the 80's and comes in clear only.

Bismarc Star—A rather heavy and attractive goblet of the 80's and clear only.

Barrel Argus — A product of the 40's and comes in clear only.

Sawtooth, Plain Stem — A pattern made during the 60's and is clear only.

Diamond Point, Coarse—A pattern made during the 60's and is clear only.

Midget New York — One of the myriad honeycomb patterns of variable age. Is to be had in light amber, blue and canary.

Plate 153

Barrel Argus   Sawtooth, Plain Stem   Diamond Point,   Midget New York
                                        Coarse

Plate 154

Clear Panels With   Stippled Bowl   Acme   Giant Baby
Cord Band   Thumbprint

Plate 155

Tile Band   Picket Band   Ripple Band   Rail Fence Band

Clear Panels With Cord Band — A pattern of the 80's and is found only in clear.

Stippled Bowl—A pattern used for many designs and produced during the 70's. Clear only.

Acme—A heavy, elaborate goblet of the 70's and has been seen only in clear.

Giant Baby Thumbprint — Socalled because of the heaviness of the pattern, created during the 60's and comes in clear only.

Tile Band — A pattern created during the 80's and comes in clear only.

Picket Band—Another goblet of the 80's and comes in clear only.

Ripple Band—A goblet of pleasing design made during the 80's and is clear only.

Rail Fence Band—A pattern of the 80's and has been found only in clear.

Texas Bull's Eye—A pattern created during the 60's and comes in clear only.

Baby Thumbprint, Four Rows — A pattern of the 80's and is found in clear only.

Belcher Loop — One of a type of goblet created from the 30's to the 60's. Clear only.

Almond Thumbprint—A product of Bakewell, Pears & Co., during the 60's and comes in clear, blue and amber.

Plate 156

Texas Bull's Eye   Baby Thumbprint   Belcher Loop   Almond, Thumbprint
                 Four Rows

Plate 157

| Way's Currant | Ostrich Looking At The Moon | Panelled Apple Blossoms | Stippled Maiden Hair Fern |

Plate 158

| Birds In Swamp | Cardinal | Beatrice | Knives And Forks |

Way's Currant—A pattern of the 80's and comes in clear only.

Ostrich Looking At The Moon—One of the many animal and fowl type of goblets made during the 80's. Clear only.

Panelled Apple Blossoms—A rather heavy and attractive goblet made during the 80's and is found only in the clear.

Stippled Maiden Hair Fern — Another goblet of the 80's and clear only.

Birds In Swamp—A pattern of the 80's and is found clear, amber. and blue.

Cardinal—A product of the 70's and comes in clear only.

Beatrice—A combination of ribs and rosettes, created in the 80's and clear only.

Knives And Forks—A goblet of the prism type, created during the 70's and clear only.

Midget Thumbprint—A product of the 90's and comes in clear only.

Doderly Thumbprint—A very heavy, clear goblet with 3 rows of large thumbprints. Made during the 80's and clear only.

Beacon Thumbprint—Another heavy goblet with single row of thumbprints. Made in 90's.

Reliable Thumbprint—A heavy, utility type of goblet. Made during the 80's and clear only.

Plate 159

Midget Thumbprint   Doderly Thumbprint   Beacon Thumbprint   Reliable Thumbprint

Plate 160

Bogatah   Acme Swirl   Charleston Swirl   Greenfield Swirl

Plate 161

Comet   Bull's Eye And   Yuma Loop   Pendleton
               Diamond Points

Bogatah — An attractive goblet of the 80's and has only been seen in clear.

Acme Swirl—A pattern of the 80's and comes in amber, clear, blue and canary.

Charleston Swirl—Another of the same period and is to be found in clear, amber, blue and canary.

Greenfield Swirl — A barrel shaped swirl of the 80's and is found in clear, amber, blue and canary.

Comet—A pattern of the 50's and comes in clear only.

Bull's Eye And Diamond Points— A heavy, attractive goblet of the 60's and comes clear only.

Yuma Loop—Another Type of the loop made during the 60's and comes in clear only.

Pendleton — An attractive goblet with very large refractive ovals, a product of the 60's and is found only in clear.

Bull's Eye, Knob Near Foot—A product of the 60's and comes in clear only.

Excelsior With Maltese Cross—As the name indicates there are maltese crosses between loops instead of concave diamonds as usual. A pattern of the 50's and comes in clear only.

Colonial, Knob Stem—A beautiful expression of this familiar pattern, produced from the 40's to the 70's, and comes clear and opaque white.

Argosy — An attractive goblet of the type usually found among the argus family, but here the loops directly oppose each other and there are two lines around bowl, a product of the 60's and comes clear only.

Plate 162

Bull's Eye, Knob Stem   Excelsior With   Colonial, Knob Stem   Argosy
    Near Foot   Maltese Cross

Plate 163

Panelled Thistle   Chandelier   Mioton With   Panelled Rosettes
                                  Almond Thumbprints

Plate 164

Diedre   Oak Leaf   Crossed Pressed Leaf   Haley's Comet

Panelled Thistle—A pattern of the 90's, but becoming scarce because of its being collected so ard arduously. Clear only.

Chandelier—A rather pleasing, slender goblet of the 80's and comes clear only.

Mioton With Almond Thumbprints And Knob Stem — A product of the 80's and comes clear only.

Panelled Rosettes—A very pleasing goblet with twisted stem and panelled rosettes on a stippled field, a product of the 80's and is found only in clear.

Diedre — A rather large, but thin glass, goblet produced during the 80's to 90's and comes in clear only.

Oak Leaf — A product of the 80's and comes in clear only.

Crossed Pressed Leaf — A pleasing goblet of the leaf type, produced during the 80's and is to be found in clear only.

Haley's Comet—A latter period of the comet and so named to distinguish it from the well known goblet of that name. It was made during the 80's and comes in clear only.

Triple Triangle, Red Top—An attractive goblet of the 80's thru the 90's and shows red top.

Royal Crystal, Red Top—Another pretty goblet of the 80's and comes with red top only.

Red Loop And Fine Cut — The loops and top are of a peculiar carmine red while the bowl generally shows well defined fine cut, produced during the 80's and may have other tints in the loops.

Frog And Spider—A rather heavy goblet with three panels, each showing a frog watching a suspended spider and on twigs overhead are two birds, a product of the 80's and comes in clear only.

Plate 165

Triple Triangle   Royal Crystal   Red Loop And   Frog And Spider
                                    Fine Cut

Plate 166

Scalloped Daisy Knobby Bull's Eye Bull's Eye & Daisies Mioton, Red Top
Red Top

Plate 167

Rosettes And Palms Brick-a-Brack Birds At Fountain Diamonds In Diamonds

Scalloped Daisy, Red Top—A product of the 90's and may show purple and gilt top.

Knobby Bull's Eye—A product of the 90's and comes with green, purple, gilt and red bull's eyes.

Bull's Eye And Daisies — Another pattern of the 90's and the bull's eyes are found in red, green, purple and gilt.

Mioton, Red Top—Another of the myriad mioton type, but with red top. A product of the 90's.

Rosettes And Palms—A goblet of the 80's and comes in clear only.

Brick-a-Brack—A very pretty goblet with highly refractive effect.

Made during the 80's and comes in clear only.

Birds At Fountain — A pattern of the 80's and comes in clear only.

Diamonds In Diamonds — A very pleasing, fairly heavy goblet of the 80's and comes in clear only.

Drapery Band With Stars—A goblet of the 80's and comes in clear only.

Clear Lion Heads — A product of the 90's and comes clear only.

Leverne—A pattern common to Pa., made in the 80's and comes in clear only.

Shield And Chain — A product of the 70's and comes in clear only.

Plate 168

Drapery Band With   Clear Lion Heads   Leverne   Shield And Chain
Stars

Plate 169

| Ohio Inverted | Utility, Knob Stem | Utility | Bennington |
| Thumbprint | | | Inverted Thumbprint |

Plate 170

| Inverted Thumbprint | Tegman Inverted | Blaze Inverted | Furgason Inverted |
| And Star | Thumbprint | Thumbprint | Thumbprint |

Ohio Inverted Thumbprint - A product of the 80's and comes in clear, amber, canary, green and blue.

Utility, Knob Stem—A heavy, plain goblet of the 70's and comes in clear only.

Utility—A plain goblet of the 70's and comes in clear only.

Bennington Inverted Thumbprint— A pattern of the 80's and comes in clear, amber, blue, green and canary.

Inverted Thumbprint With Star— A product of the 80's and comes in clear, amber, blue, green and canary.

Tegman Inverted Thumbprint — A product of the 80's and comes in clear, amber, blue, green and canary.

Blaze Inverted Thumbprint — A product of the 80's and comes in clear, amber, blue, green and canary.

Furgason Inverted Thumbprint—A product of the 80's and comes in clear, amber, blue, green and canary.

Quantico — A beaded band goblet with wild flowers on the bowl, made in the 80's and comes in clear only.

Square Daisy And Button—A product of the 80's and comes in clear, amber, blue and canary.

Prince Albert — A tall, squarish type of daisy and button which was made during the 90's and comes in clear, amber, blue and canary.

Dinner Bell—A product of the 80's and comes in clear only.

Plate 171

| Quantico | Square Daisy And Button | Prince Albert | Dinner Bell |

Plate 172

Bissing   Reardon   Elator   Cocoon Band

Plate 173

Stippled Fleur de Lis   Curtain   Double Spear   Panelled Stippled
                                                            Scroll

Bissing — A plain type of goblet with fluted lower bowl, a product of the 90's and is found only in clear.

Reardon—A very pretty, sparkling goblet of the 80's and comes in clear only.

Elator—A clear, thin type of goblet with short loops at bottom of the bowl and a nice knobbed stem, made in the 80's and clear only.

Cocoon Band—An attractive banded goblet of the 90's and comes clear only.

Stippled Fleur de Lis—A pattern of the 80's and comes n amber, blue and green.

Curtain—A pattern of the 70's and comes in clear only.

Double Spear — A pattern of the 80's and comes in clear only.

Panelled Stippled Scroll — A pattern of the 70's and comes in amber, green and blue.

Cantilever Band—A product of the 80's and comes in clear only.

Fine Tooth Band—A pretty goblet with fine ribbed band and knob stem, made during the 90's and comes in clear only.

Aberdeen — A pattern of the 80's and comes in clear only.

Curlew—A pattern with design low on the bowl and of rather faint imprint, made during the 80's and is found in clear only.

Plate 174

Cantilever Band   Finetooth Band   Aberdeen   Curlew

Plate 175

| Paling | Chain | Chain With Star | Picket |

Plate 176

| Cape Cod | Frosted Waffle | Oswego Waffle | Diamond Sunburst |

Paling—A pattern of the 80's and comes clear only.

Chain — A pattern of the 80's and clear only.

Chain With Star—A pattern of the 80's and comes in clear only.

Picket—A pattern of the 80's and comes clear only.

Cape Cod — A pattern of the 70's and is found in clear only.

Frosted Waffle—A pattern of the 80's and comes in clear only.

Oswego Waffle — A heavy waffle type with bowl entirely covered to near top and without bars. Pattern of the 80's and clear only.

Diamond Sunburst — A pattern of the 80's and is found in clear only.

Spirea Band—A pleasing goblet of the 80's and is to be found in clear only.

Fans, With Baby Breath Band— One of the usual clea panelled goblets with fans and this one has a delicate band of baby breath. Period of the 80's and comes in clear only.

Daisy And Button, With Block Band —A product of the 90's and comes in clear only.

Panelled Night Shade — A very pretty, sparkling goblet of the 80's and comes in clear only.

Plate 177

Spirea Band   Fans, With Baby Breath Band   Daisy And Button With Block Band   Panelled Night Shade

GLOSSARY

A

Aberdeen, Plate 174.
Acme, Plate 154.
Acme Swirl, Plate 160.
Acorn, Plate 114.
Actress, Plate 121.
Almond Thumbprint, Plate 156.
Amberino, Plate 75.
Amulet, Plate 150.
Anheuser Busch "A," Plate 120.
Anheuser Busch "Faust," Plate 120.
Arab, Plate 130.
Arabesque, Plate 130.
Arched Grape, Plate 51.
Arched Leaf, Plate 94.
Argosy, Plate 162.
Art, Plate 108.
Ashman, Plate 119.
Aster Band, Plate 49.

B

Baby Face, Plate 149.
Baby Thumbprint, 4 Rows, Plate 156.
Balder, Plate 14.
Balloon, Plate 107.
Baltimore Pear, Plate 86.
Banded Buckle, Plate 110.
Banded Cube, Plate 135.
Banded Icicle, Plate 102.
Banded Vernon, Plate 9.
Barberry, Oval Berries, Plate 59.
Barberry, Round Berries, Plate 59.
Barley, Plate 97.
Barred Daisy, Plate 27.
Barred For-get-me-not, Plate 140.
Barrel Argus, Plate 153.
Barrel Ashburton, Plate 6.
Barrel Excelsior, Plate 19.
Barrel Huber, Plate 21.
Barrel Thumbprint, Plate 1.
Bartlett Pear, Plate 59.
Basket Weave, Plate 127.
Beacon Thumbprint, Plate 159.
Beaded Acorn, Plate 85.
Beaded Band, Plate 97.
Beaded Dewdrop, Plate 119.
Beaded Frog's Eye, Plate 141.
Beaded Grape, Plate 79.
Beaded Grape Medallion, Plate 85.
Beaded Grape Medallion, Banded, Plate 85.
Beaded Grape Medallion, Design On Foot, Plate 85.
Beaded Loop, Plate 82.
Beaded Oval And Scroll, Plate 119.
Beaded Oval Windows, Plate 91.
Beaded Ovals, Plate 47.
Beaded Rosettes, Plate 14.
Beaded Tulip, Plate 124.

Beadle, Plate 83.
Beatrice, Plate 158.
Bee Hive, Plate 122.
Belcher Loop, Plate 156.
Bellflower, Coarse Rib, Straight Sides, Rayed Base, Plate 16.
Bellflower, Fine Rib, Band At Top, Plate 94.
Bellflower, Fine Rib, Knob Stem, Barrel Shape, Plain Base, Plate 16.
Bellflower, Fine Rib, Plain Stem, Plate 13.
Belt Buckle, Plate 109.
Bennington Inverted Thumbprint, Plate 169.
Bessimer Flute, Plate 4.
Bigler, Plate 21.
Birds At Fountain, Plate 167.
Birds In Swamp, Plate 158.
Bismarc Star, Plate 152.
Bissing, Plate 172.
Blaze, Plate 76.
Blaze Inverted Thumbprint, Plate 170.
Bleeding Heart, Knob Stem, Plate 43.
Bleeding Heart, Plain Stem, Plate 43.
Block And Circle, Plate 113.
Block And Double Bar, Plate 136.
Block And Fan, Plate 135.
Block And Jewel, Plate 105.
Block And Spear Point, Plate 96.
Block And Thumbprint, Knob Stem, Plate 117.
Block And Thumbprint, Plate 126.
Block House, Plate 133.
Block With Sawtooth Band, Plate 136.
Blucher, Plate 150.
Bogatah, Plate 160.
Bohemian Red, Vintage Pattern, Plate 145.
Bouquet, Plate 62.
Bradford Grape, Plate 15.
Brick-a-Brack, Plate 167.
Brilliant, Plate 125.
Broken Column, Plate 139.
Brooklyn, Plate 131.
Brooklyn Flute, Plate 4.
Buckle, Plate 110.
Buckle With Star, Plate 110.
Budded Ivy, Plate 47.
Bull's Eye And Daisies, Plate 166.
Bull's Eye And Diamond Panels, Plate 109.
Bull's Eye And Diamond Points, Plate 161.
Bull's Eye And Spear Head, Plate 45.
Bull's Eye In Hearts, Plate 63.
Bull's Eye, Knob In Centre Of Stem, Plate 87.
Bull's Eye, Knob Near Bowl, Plate 34.
Bull's Eye, Knob Stem Near Foot, Plate 162.
Bumble Bee Honeycomb, Plate 9.
Bungalow, Plate 24.
Butterfly And Fan, Plate 140.

C

Cabbage Rose, Plate 52.
Cable, Plate 37.
Canadian, Plate 35.
Cane, Plate 122.
Cannon Ball, Plate 88.
Cantilever Band, Plate 174.
Cape Cod, Plate 176.
Cardinal, Plate 158.
Cat 'O Nine Tails And Ferns, Plate 141.

D

F

Fairfax Strawberry, Plate 31.
Falcon Strawberry, Plate 52.
Fans With Baby Breath Band, Plate 177.
Fan With Diamonds, Plate 64.
Feather, Plate 30.
Fedora Loop, Knob Stem, Plate 22.
Ferris Wheel, Plate 50.
Festoon And Grape, Stippled Leaf, Plate 51.
Festoon And Grape, Veined Leaf, Plate 148.
Fibber Block, Plate 90.
Fine Cut, Plate 110.
Fine Cut And Block, Plate 28.
Fine Cut And Panel, Plate 89.
Fine Rib To Top, Plate 148.
Fine Rib, Plain Band At Top, Plate 75.
Fine Tooth Band, Plate 174.
Fish Scale, Plate 87.
Flack, Plate 147.
Flat Prisms, Plate 23.
Flat Prisms (Barrel Shape), Plate 100.
Flame, Plate 88.
Flamingo, Plate 61.
Flare Top Excelsior, Plate 19.
Flare Top Worchester, Belted, Plate 6.
Flaring Huber, Plate 21.
Flattened Hobnail, Plate 33.
Fleur de Lis, Plate 97.
Florida Palm, Plate 95.
Fluted Icicle, Plate 75.
Flying Birds, Plate 111.
Flying Robin, Plate 101.
For-get-me-not In Scroll, Plate 86.
Frazier, Plate 115.
Fretted Vault, Plate 108.
Frog And Spider, Plate 165.
Frosted Actress, Plate 80.
Frosted Circle, Plate 94.
Frosted Festal Ball, Plate 149.
Frosted Flower Band, Plate 74.
Frosted Leaf, Plate 114.
Frosted Lion, Plate 149.
Frosted Magnolia, Plate 99.
Frosted Circle, Plate 134.
Frosted Polar Bear, Plate 73.
Frosted Ribbon, Plate 37.
Frosted Roman Key With Flutes, Plate 143.
Frosted Roman Key With Ribs, Plate 72.
Frosted Stork, Plate 61.
Frosted Waffle, Plate 176.
Fruit Panels, Plate 60.
Furgason Inverted Thumbprint, Plate 170.

G

G. A. R., Plate 80.
Galloway, Plate 7.
Gandy Strawberry; Plate 60.
Garden Fern, Plate 44.
Garfield Drape, Plate 133.
Geddes, Plate 49.
Georgia Belle, Plate 56.
Giant Ashburton, Plate 5.
Giant Baby Thumbprint, Plate 154.

N

O

P

Q

R

S

Y

Z